Bounty Hunter

VIRGINIA LOH-HAGAN

⊖ 45th Parallel Press

Published in the United States of America by Cherry Lake Publishing
Ann Arbor, Michigan
www.cherrylakepublishing.com

Content Adviser: Dawn Baird, Bail Agent
Reading Adviser: Reading Adviser: Marla Conn MS, Ed., Literacy specialist,
Read-Ability, Inc.

Photo Credits: © www.BillionPhotos.com/Shutterstock, cover, 1; © Kzenon/Shutterstock, 5; © vlad.georgescu/
Shutterstock, 6; ©ncognet0/istock, 9; © Chris Johnson/Thinkstock, 11; © Elena Dijour/Shutterstock, 13;
© Wavebreak/istock, 14; © IgorGolovniov/Shutterstock, 17; © Mike Powell/Thinkstock, 19; © moodboard/
Thinkstock, 21; © Douglas R. Clifford/ZUMApress/Newscom, 23; © bikeriderlondon/Shutterstock, 25;
© Photographee.eu/Shutterstock, 26; © Burlingham/Shutterstock, 28; © ARENA Creative/Shutterstock,
cover, multiple interior pages; © oculo/Shutterstock, multiple interior pages; © Denniro/Shutterstock.com,
cover, multiple interior pages; © PhotoHouse/Shutterstock, multiple interior pages; © Miloje/Shutterstock,
multiple interior pages

45th Parallel Press is an imprint of Cherry Lake Publishing.

Library of Congress Cataloging-in-Publication Data

Names: Loh-Hagan, Virginia, author.
Title: Bounty hunter / by Virginia Loh-Hagan.
Description: Ann Arbor : Cherry Lake Pub., 2016. I Series: Odd jobs I
  Includes bibliographical references and index.
Identifiers: LCCN 2015049878I ISBN 9781634710947 (hbk) I ISBN 9781634712927
  (pbk) I ISBN 9781634711937 (pdf) I ISBN 9781634713917 (ebk)
Subjects: LCSH: Bounty hunters—Juvenile literature.
Classification: LCC HV8099.5 .L64 2016 I DDC 363.28—dc23
LC record available at http://lccn.loc.gov/2015049878

Cherry Lake Publishing would like to acknowledge the work of The Partnership for 21st Century Skills.
Please visit *www.p21*.org for more information.

Printed in the United States of America
Corporate Graphics Inc.

Contents

CHAPTER 1

Human Hunters

Who's Bob Burton? How is bounty hunting dangerous? Who's David Marshburn?

Bob Burton hunts people. Then, he **arrests** them. Arrest means taking someone to jail. He's a **bounty** hunter. He also trains bounty hunters. A bounty is a money award. Bounty hunters get paid for finding **fugitives**. Fugitives fled from the law. They're also called targets.

Burton has arrested over 3,200 people. He's done odd things. He dressed as a rabbit. Odd things happened to him. A target threw poop at him.

He has a special move. He finds his target. He talks about friendly things. He asks, "Do you like chocolate sandwiches?" This causes confusion. Then, he makes his arrest.

Fugitives are also known as outlaws.

Burton's hunt begins when he's hired. He researches. He gets personal information. He does a **stakeout**. Staking out takes awhile. He waits hours. He waits days. He learns about the target's habits. He finds **informants.** Informants have information. Burton pays them. Then, they tell him things.

Some targets committed small crimes. They don't tend to be dangerous. Burton talks to them. He asks them to turn themselves in.

Stakeouts can take days. Bounty hunters must be ready for anything.

Spotlight Biography
LEONARD PADILLA

Leonard Padilla is a bounty hunter. He lives in Sacramento, California. He tracks down fugitives. He tracks down remains of murder victims. Remains are what's left of dead bodies. He wears a black western shirt. He wears black pants. He wears a black cowboy hat with a feather. He has appeared on television talk shows and movies. Padilla is known for being a "straight shooter." This means he's honest. His first bounty hunt was in 1975. He went to Mexico. He found a fugitive. He brought him back to the United States. He realized he could make good money doing this. He went to law school. He ran for mayor several times. He still loves bounty hunting. He said, "It's the challenge of coming up with a solution to a problem nobody has been able to come up with."

Some targets committed big crimes. They may fight back. Burton distracts them. He jams car locks. He does this with paper. Targets fumble around. This gives him time to act.

Targets don't like bounty hunters. They don't want to be caught. Sometimes, they attack. Ray Hawkins is a bounty hunter. He's been shot. He's been stabbed. He's been run over by a car.

Targets hide from bounty hunters. They're scared of David Marshburn. They've hidden in cabinets. They've hidden in sofa beds. They've hidden in fridges.

Marshburn travels a lot. One of his targets was a drug lord. Marshburn followed him. He took nine trips to Florida. He took two trips to Arizona. He took two trips to Massachusetts. He has fun. He said, "I love getting up every day knowing this is what I do for a living."

Fugitives are often dangerous.

CHAPTER 2

Hunting Bounties

How does bounty hunting work? How are bounty hunters and cops alike and different? What do bounty hunters do?

Bounty hunting involves four main people. Targets are accused of a crime. They wait to go to court. They're sent to jail. Targets don't want to stay in jail. They pay **bail**. Bail is money. Doing so releases them from jail. They promise to appear in court. Some targets **skip** bail. This means they run away. They try to skip their court dates.

Judges set the bail. They set high bails for **flight risks**. Flight risks are people. They're more likely to skip.

Sometimes, the targets can't pay bail. They don't have the money. **Bail bondsmen** loan them money. They charge extra fees. They lose money when targets skip. So they hire bounty hunters. Bounty hunters capture these targets. They return them to court. Then, they get paid.

Sometimes, more than one bounty hunter may be assigned to a case.

Targets cost a lot of money. They take up a lot of time. They break laws. Bounty hunters help. They bring targets to justice.

Targets sign **contracts** with bail bondsmen. They make an agreement. Targets accept bail money. In return, they give away their rights. They know they will be hunted if they skip.

Bounty hunters are different from cops. They don't have as many rules. They're more successful. They find 90 percent of targets. They have better resources. Some make more money.

Cops can't chase all targets. They have too much to do. They can't leave the state. The **FBI** only chases really dangerous cases. That's the Federal Bureau of Investigation. So, bounty hunters are needed. They take any and all cases.

Bounty hunters use tools. They're spies. Some use disguises. Some have vans. They put fake signs on the vans. The vans transport targets. They contain spy gear. They have cameras. They have radios. They have special goggles. The goggles help them see in the dark.

Bounty hunters work long hours. They work all the time.

Bounty hunters can't hurt targets. But they need to defend themselves. They restrain targets. Some use pepper spray. Some carry shotguns. Some carry police sticks. Some wear bulletproof vests.

They use the element of surprise. This is their greatest weapon. They show up late at night. They show up at weird places. They pretend to be someone else.

Bounty hunters can investigate in ways the police cannot.

Bounty Hunter
KNOW THE LINGO

Arraigned: being formally charged with a crime

Bail jumping: someone on bail who doesn't go to court

Bail piece: paperwork indicating that the person is a fugitive

Busted: arrested

Collateral: a person's property that is equal in value to a money loan

Custody: when an arrested person is taken by the police

FTA: "failure to appear," skipping out on bail

Going down: going to jail

Inkman: a forger, someone who makes false identification papers

Judas: a person who tells bounty hunters where fugitives are hiding

Midnight run: an easy capture

Pull leather: helping other bounty hunters

Recovery: bringing someone back to the authorities

Skip tracing: the act of tracking someone down

Troll: a fugitive who's hiding

Warrant: official legal permission

CHAPTER 3

Becoming a Bounty Hunter

What do states regulate? What's needed to become a bounty hunter?

Each state has its own rules. Bounty hunters need to follow laws. Some states require training. Some require **licenses**. Licenses are official permission. They let people do things. Some states don't require anything. Bounty hunters just need to be hired. Bondsmen hire them.

Some states **ban** bounty hunting. Ban means to not allow. Some states restrict bounty hunting. They limit what bounty hunters can do.

Many states allow bounty hunters to enter targets' homes. They don't need court permission. But bounty hunters have to be sure the target is there. They need to do careful research.

Bounty hunters can't hunt outside of the United States. This law is serious. They can be arrested. They can be shot.

Some states have schools. Some groups provide workshops and classes. But the best training is learning from others.

Bounty hunters need to be fit. They run. They learn self-defense. They fight. They use weapons.

They need to be smart. They're sneaky. They investigate. They make quick decisions.

Advice From the Field
JOHN DOYLE

John Doyle is retired. He was a bounty hunter for 14 years. He's 6 foot 3 inches (190.5 centimeters). He played football. He was a soldier. He thinks bounty hunters should work as a team. It's safer. It allows bounty hunters to cover different escape routes. He hires bounty hunters who are team players. He doesn't like "cowboys." Cowboys are bounty hunters who show off. They like power. They think they're above the law. He said, "You can spot [the cowboys] pretty quickly. If you're in a public place, they've got the badge hanging from their neck, a gun hanging from their hip, three or four pairs of handcuffs hanging that everybody can see." Good bounty officers need to be able to work with different people.

Staying fit is important for good bounty hunters.

Bounty hunters need to be good interviewers. They talk to targets' friends. They talk to family members. They talk to neighbors. They talk to anyone who knows the targets. They need people skills.

They need to work under pressure. They have limited time. They have to return targets to court. They also need patience. They need time to find people. They have to be able to wait.

CHAPTER 4

Wild West to Today

How did bounty hunting develop? What are the major laws related to bounty hunting?

The *Bounty* was a British ship. Rebels took it over. This happened in 1789. Captain Edward Edwards captured these rebels. He's known as the first bounty hunter.

Bails started in England. They started in the 13th century. At that time, *bail* referred to a person. Bails took responsibility for prisoners. Sometimes, prisoners ran away. Bails took their place. They took the prisoners' punishment. Some were even hanged.

Bounty hunters were popular in the Wild West. They were called gunslingers. They chased **outlaws**. Outlaws are fugitives. Bounty hunters looked for "Wanted" posters. These showed the outlaws. They listed reward money.

Some posters used to read, "Wanted: Dead or Alive." Today, bounty hunters can only bring back fugitives alive.

WHEN ODD IS TOO ODD!

The Lipstick Bounty Hunters is a group of female bounty hunters. They're former Los Angeles police officers. They wear pink. They have pink handcuffs. They have pink guns. They were tracking Daniel Duvall. Duvall had drug and weapons charges. The Lipstick Bounty Hunters found him in a fast food restaurant. They swarmed him. They shot him with a stun gun. They shot him with rubber bullets. They filmed this. They posted the video online. People thought they were too aggressive. Duvall said they broke his nose, blinded him, bruised him, and cut him. Teresa Golt is the leader. She said, "We don't know of any other female bounty hunters in California. We have our own style and we always get our man…What we do works for us, and 90 percent of people we arrest are very happy with us." Duvall isn't part of the 90 percent.

There are laws about bounty hunting. The Eighth Amendment is part of the Constitution. It ensures that bail money is a reasonable amount.

Taylor versus Taintor happened in 1872. It's a Supreme Court case. It gives bounty hunters power. It treats them like cops. It lets them arrest people who skip bail. It lets them chase targets across states. It lets them break into houses. It lets them capture targets. They don't have to read targets their rights. But states can decide differently. They can make their own laws.

Some prisoners are too dangerous. They shouldn't be released on bail. They should stay in jail. The Bail Reform Act happened in 1984. It lets courts hold prisoners without bail.

Bounty hunters are part of the law enforcement system.

CHAPTER 5

Trouble with Hunting Humans

What are some issues or challenges of bounty hunting? How is bounty hunting changing?

Timm Johnson and Daniel Kear are bounty hunters. They captured Sidney Jaffe. Jaffe was near his home. He lived in Canada. Johnson and Kear found him. They took him to Florida. They did their job. But they got in trouble. They were accused of kidnapping.

Bounty hunters get in trouble. Sometimes, they break laws. Some targets flee across states. Some flee to different countries.

This job isn't easy. Bounty hunters find criminals. Sometimes, targets aren't nice. Bounty hunters have been arrested for hurting targets. They've been arrested for having guns. They've been arrested for bullying.

Bounty hunters can be arrested for pretending to be cops.

Jackie Shell is a bounty hunter. He tracked down Randy Howard. Howard sang country music. He skipped bail. Shell went to his house. Howard shot at him. Shell shot back. He killed Howard. Shell got hurt. He healed. But he got in trouble. People questioned Shell's actions. They questioned bounty hunting.

Not everyone agrees with bounty hunting. They want to stop bounty hunting.

THAT HAPPENED?!?

Brent Farley was tracking a fugitive. He put the fugitive's picture on social media. He got a tip. Farley went to a house in Phoenix, Arizona. It was late at night. Farley and other bounty hunters staked out the house for two hours. Farley banged on the door. He shouted. He shined lights into the house. He carried a gun. He was at the wrong house. It was the chief of police's house! Chief Joseph Yahner was mad. Farley was arrested. He wasn't licensed. He was charged with disorderly conduct. He was also charged with criminal trespassing. Farley said he should've done more research. He said, "I'm getting out of the business after this." Aaron Bray gave Farley the bad tip! Bray is a rival bounty hunter. He wanted to mess with Farley. Bray was arrested for being reckless.

It's hard for fugitives to stay hidden in the Information Age.

Some bounty hunters capture the wrong people. James Howard Dickerson is a bounty hunter. He was chasing a target. He broke down the door. He dragged out Roberto Martinez. Martinez tried to escape. Dickerson shot him. He killed him. But he got the wrong guy! He went to the wrong house! Dickerson was arrested. The state added more laws.

Technology is changing bounty hunting. **Drones** can search for people. Drones are like tiny planes. Computers track data. They identify faces. They update faces. Bounty hunters use the Web. They track targets. They use social media. They have better cameras. They have better tracking devices. Technology makes their job easier.

Bounty hunting has been around forever. It keeps changing. But justice workers are always needed.

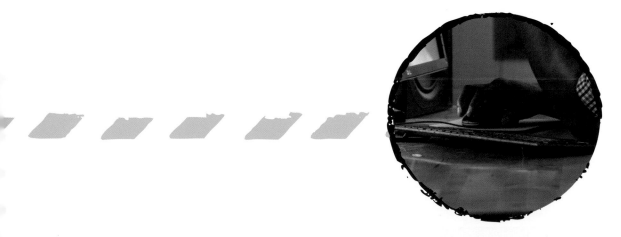

DID YOU KNOW?

- Bounty hunters are also known as bail bond enforcers, fugitive recovery agents, skip tracers, or fugitive apprehension specialists.

- There aren't many female bounty hunters. But women can be good bounty hunters. People trust women more. They tell women more things.

- Some states allow former criminals to become bounty hunters.

- Dog the Bounty Hunter had his own television show. But he isn't a real bounty hunter. He's not allowed to arrest anyone. He's not allowed to carry a gun. He uses pepper spray.

- Boba Fett is a popular fictional bounty hunter. He's in *Star Wars*. He captured Han Solo. He brought Solo to Jabba the Hutt.

- Raj Rajaratnam had one of the highest bails in U.S. history. His bail was $100 million. He cheated people out of a lot of money.

- Harriet Tubman was a famous fugitive. She was a slave. She escaped to the North. She helped other slaves escape. She eluded bounty hunters. Her bounty was over $40,000. (This was a lot of money during the Civil War era.)

- The average bounty hunter gets 100 contracts a year.

- Some fugitives have several bounty hunters hunting them. Most bounty hunters reject these contracts. They don't want the competition.

- Simon Barrett has a radio program. It's on Blog Talk Radio. It's titled, "America's Most Unwanted and the People Who Find Them."

CONSIDER THIS!

TAKE A POSITION! Some people think the bail system is unfair. They think it's unfair to poor people. They also think it's dangerous to let people act like cops without rules. Do you think bounty hunting is still needed today? Argue your point with reasons and evidence.

SAY WHAT? Explain how bounty hunters are different from police officers. Explain how bounty hunters are similar to police officers.

THINK ABOUT IT! There have been several reality television shows about bounty hunters. Why do you think people like watching these shows? Why is bounty hunting exciting to watch?

SEE A DIFFERENT SIDE! Not all bounty hunters serve the law. Zena Briggs was being forced to marry. She didn't want to. So, she ran away. Her family hired a bounty hunter to find her. She doesn't like bounty hunters. Why do you think this is so? How can some bounty hunters be unhelpful?

LEARN MORE: RESOURCES

PRIMARY SOURCE
Burton, Bob. *Bounty Hunter*. Boulder, CO: Paladin Press, 1984.

SECONDARY SOURCES
Cefrey, Holly. *Bounty Hunters*. New York: Scholastic, 2003.
Donkin, Andrew. *Crime Busters*. New York: DK Publishing, 2001.
Owen, David. *Police Lab: How Forensic Science Tracks Down and Convicts Criminals*. Toronto: Firefly Books, 2002.

WEB SITES
National Association of Bail Enforcement Agents: www.nabea.org
National Association of Fugitive Recovery Agents: www.fugitive-recovery.org

GLOSSARY

arrests (uh-RESTS) takes someone to jail

bail (BAYL) the sum of money paid to a court to allow someone accused of a crime to be set free until his or her trial

bail bondsmen (BAYL BAHNDZ-mun) people who loan money or bail to the accused

ban (BAN) to not allow

bounty (BOUN-tee) a reward offered for the capture of a fugitive

contracts (KAHN-trakts) agreements between bondsmen and targets

drones (DROHNZ) unmanned aerial vehicles

FBI (EFF-BEE-IY) the Federal Bureau of Investigation, a government crime fighting organization

flight risks (FLITE RISKS) people who are more likely to skip bail

fugitives (FYOO-ji-tivz) people who are running away from the police; outlaws

informants (in-FOR-mantz) people who reveal information

licenses (LYE-suhns-iz) official permission or certificates to do something

outlaws (OUT-lawz) fugitives

skip (SKIP) ignore or flee

stakeout (STAYK-out) watching a place

INDEX

ABOUT THE AUTHOR

Dr. Virginia Loh-Hagan is an author, university professor, former classroom teacher, and curriculum designer. She's a hunter of good hot dogs, not bounties. She lives in San Diego with her very tall husband and very naughty dogs. To learn more about her, visit www.virginialoh.com.